Corinne Sweet is a psychologist, psychotherapist, and author of nonfiction titles including *The Anxiety Journal* and *Change Your Life with CBT*. A journalist and broadcaster, she is a well-respected figure in self-help, and mindfulness is one of her specialist areas.

Marcia Mihotich is a London-based graphic designer and illustrator whose clients include The School of Life, Donna Wilson, and the *Guardian*. She is also creative director of Rosy Lee Tea London.

D0027318

THE MINDFULNESS JOURNAL

*Exercises to help you find peace
and calm wherever you are*

CORINNE SWEET

Illustrated by
Marcia Mihotich

Published in the United States by Rodale Books, an imprint of Random House, a division of Penguin Random House LLC, New York.
rodalebooks.com

RODALE and the Plant colophon are registered trademarks of Penguin Random House LLC.

Originally published in the United Kingdom by Boxtree, an imprint of Pan Macmillan, a division of Macmillan Publishers Limited in 2014.

Quotation references are located on pages 221–222.

Library of Congress Cataloging-in-Publication Data is a available upon request.

ISBN 978-0-593-23320-7

Printed in the United States of America

Book design and illustrations by Marcia Mihotich
Cover design by Black Kat Design
Cover art by chamanbhai tala/Digital Vision Vectors/Getty Images

10 9 8 7 6 5 4 3 2 1

First U.S. Edition

To Joan (1928–2013) and
Leslie Sweet (1916–1996), who
made me realize the importance
of living in the now

WHAT IS MINDFULNESS?

Take a moment to stop.
Notice your posture.
Be aware of your breathing.
Can you feel your body?
Do you feel any pain or strain anywhere?
Is your mind racing? Or are you calm?
Are you comfortable? Or a bit tense?
Too hot? Cold? Just right?
Are you hungry or thirsty?
What are you actually feeling this second?
Irritable? Happy? Sad? Bored? Relaxed?

This is what mindfulness is about.

Mindfulness is about being completely IN THE NOW. It's about noticing, *this second*, how you feel, what you think, what you want, without criticism or judgment.

It's about learning to notice everything in your body, your mind, and your environment: the gurgles in your stomach, the twitches in your back, the clenching of your jaw, the rain on the window, the clouds in the sky, the purring of your cat, the flowers in the garden, the smile of your child, the sound of a far-off train, the traffic on the street, a bird twittering on a branch, the itch on your nose, the whirr of your computer, or the taste of a melting square of chocolate on your tongue.

Mindfulness is about noticing everything in the moment.

It's about learning to focus your attention in the present.

This very second. This millisecond. **NOW.**

It's about **living in present time.**

Paradox lost

This seems a very simple thing to do. And yet it seems quite difficult to master for many of us.

It takes effort. It takes decision. It takes regular practice.

The paradox is: *something very simple can be quite difficult to do.*

But in time, with regular, daily practice, that paradox is lost as you gradually gain the skill.

Mindfully.

Mindfulness is:
* about being present
* a way to focus on now
* a way to calm your thoughts down
* an effective means of relaxing
* a way to release your creativity
* a way to boost physical and emotional health
* a way to gain compassion and empathy

WHY BE MINDFUL?

There is a growing body of evidence—psychological, physiological, scientific—that our 24/7, chaotic, pressurized, stress-filled lives are doing us immense harm.

Many of us are suffering from mental and physical health issues that can be helped significantly by taking the time to slow down and learn, simply, to breathe.

Mindfulness can help you become calmer, more peaceful, and focused.

Mindfulness is not about eliminating stress, as stress is a given in life, but it can help us deal with stress and other challenges more effectively. It has been proven to help relieve stress, anxiety, and depression and can even relieve some of the symptoms of ailments such as chronic fatigue syndrome, eating disorders, cancer, chronic pain, and sleep disorders.

Mindfulness is now recognized by NICE (the National Institute for Health and Care Excellence) in the UK as an effective form of therapy for dealing with physical and psychological stress. As a consequence, GPs, hospitals, parenting organizations, schools, social services, and other government departments are offering mindfulness training and helping people to learn to meditate. Meditation helps slow the mind down and enables it to focus calmly on the here and now, and therefore is the chief, conscious route to achieving a state of mindfulness.

MINDFULNESS AND
COGNITIVE THERAPY

In the East, mindfulness and meditation have been a practice of Buddhism for nearly 3,000 years, and over the past two centuries these ideas have spread to the West. Meditation became associated with the hippy counterculture movement of the 1960s and 1970s, but its benefits later percolated into mainstream society through New Age and other complementary therapies, such as alternative medicine and yoga practices.

In the West, the rise of "talking therapies" in the early twentieth century, such as the psychoanalysis of Freud and Jung, and later the behaviorism of Skinner and Ellis, offered people a way to make sense of their difficulties and pressures. From these two approaches, the humanistic branch of psychotherapy evolved, with therapies such as gestalt, person-centered, and psychosynthesis. This kind of work is usually done with individual therapists or in groups.

A lot of these therapies focus on understanding your past as a way of getting beyond it; in the oft-quoted words of Socrates: "The unexamined life is not worth living." However, many people now think there is also major value in putting the therapeutic focus on the present, rather than the past, as a way of moving forward effectively.

In the twenty-first century, CBT (Cognitive Behavioral Therapy) has become a popular way of helping people deal with anxiety, depression, stress, and addictions. CBT is often seen as a way of developing a forward-looking mental muscle to deal with everyday issues. It combats negative thinking and supports individual responsibility. It also provides shorter, goal-based solutions, rather than long-term psychotherapeutic "talking therapy." CBT can be available via referral from your GP and there are private practitioners available for most types of psychotherapy and CBT. These can be very effective, especially as a way of solving an immediate and pressing problem, such as an addiction or obsessive thinking.

The evolving fusion of Eastern and Western practices and therapies led to the creation of Mindfulness-based Cognitive Therapy (MBCT) and Mindfulness-based Stress Reduction (MBSR), which have been proven to be extremely effective in reducing anxiety, depression, addiction, pain, illness, and stress. MBCT is a way of retraining your mind to operate in a different way, drawing on techniques from Buddhism and meditation. MBSR also makes use of yoga techniques. Both of these practices emphasize direct personal experience of specific exercises. These are the exercises you will learn in this book. The more you do the exercises, the more mindful, and relaxed, you will become.

The good news is that you can learn to do this for yourself, from this book, today.

Mindfulness can help you enormously, and practice is totally free.

WHY IS MINDFULNESS GROWING IN POPULARITY?

A key figure in developing this area is Jon Kabat-Zinn, who started a stress-reduction clinic at the University of Massachusetts Medical School in 1979. He was a molecular biologist who gave up his scientific career to bring his experience of Zen meditation and yoga practices to help sick patients.

Kabat-Zinn wanted to see if patients could improve, physically and mentally, as a result of teaching them to meditate. He also wanted to bring mindfulness meditation—the tenet of Buddhist practice—to a wider Western audience.

His book *Full Catastrophe Living* describes his pioneering work and the astonishing results he achieved from teaching mindfulness meditation to people with chronic illness, stress, and pain.

WHAT PROOF IS THERE
THAT IT WORKS?

There is growing scientific evidence of the effectiveness of mindfulness. Studies around the world have shown that with regular meditation:

* anxiety and depression decrease
* immunity to colds, flu, and other diseases is boosted
* chronic pain, even from cancer, can be reduced
* feelings of "happiness" and "positivity" increase, and regular meditators are more contented than average
* stress and stressors leading to hypertension and heart disease can be relieved
* concentration, memory, and physical stamina are increased

Overall, it is thought that the "positive" effects of mindfulness meditation can lead to a longer and healthier life.

HOW DO I BEGIN?

You can start with just five minutes. You need a timer, a high-backed chair, and a quiet space.

Basic meditation

Go to your quiet space and make it clear to others that you don't want to be disturbed. Put a sign on the door. Put your phone on silent. Set a timer for 5 minutes.

Sit comfortably with your back supported and your hands resting on your thighs or comfortably in your lap. Close your eyes. Breathe in slowly and think "rising" as the air comes in through your nose. Breathe out slowly and think "falling" as the air goes out through your mouth. Focus your mind's attention just behind the midpoint of your forehead.

Continue breathing in and out, thinking "rising" on the in, "falling" on the out. Notice background sounds as you breathe, and just let them go. Continue breathing in and out, thinking "rising" and "falling." If you feel an itch or a twitch, don't scratch—let it go. When your mind wanders, bring it gently back to the central point behind your forehead.

When the timer goes off, gently open your eyes. Take a second to notice how you feel. Stretch your arms and legs, get to your feet and stretch again. Pause for a second. Tune in to your body, your feelings, your mind. How do you feel?

REGULAR DAILY PRACTICE

Start small.

Try this basic meditation five minutes a day for a week. Then move up to ten minutes, and then fifteen minutes. Once the technique becomes more familiar, you may want to practice for half an hour and then an hour.

One of the most important parts of the mindfulness meditation is returning your attention to the midpoint behind your forehead. It is this activity that helps to build new neural pathways in the brain—it literally retrains your mind to be more focused and calm.

This is just one basic meditation exercise to help you get started. As you progress, there are other ways to be mindful through other meditations, visualizations, and activities. Eventually, you'll be able to take a five-minute meditation break whenever and wherever you feel the need to focus.

You can increase or decrease the time and choose exercises suited to your situation, whether you're in the car, on the train, walking, having a sleepless night, in a doctor's waiting room, or arriving at work—anywhere you feel under duress and in need of calm. Set aside time, and stick to it.

Know yourself: be realistic about when and how to practice. Set your alarm and get out of bed ten minutes earlier, or meditate in bed before you go to sleep once all your chores are done.

You may feel you haven't got time for it. However, once you get into the habit, you will find the rewards will motivate you to take that little bit of time out of your day to make it go better overall.

If you find it hard to concentrate, don't worry. Don't give up. This is a new skill, and it takes time to get used to it. You didn't ride a bike the minute you sat on it. You had to learn to swim or drive a car. Give yourself time to get used to the process, and you'll soon get into the swing of it. Be patient with yourself as you learn.

Just give it a go. Then try it again. And again. Soon you'll be doing it, and enjoying it.

Stick with it

Regularity is essential. All the evidence points to regularity being the key to gaining benefits. It is the accumulative effect of slowing down your mind, and calming anxiety and repetitive or obtrusive thoughts, that is so powerful.

If you miss a day, don't beat yourself up. Approach your mindfulness meditation with a positive and kind attitude towards yourself.

Don't judge or punish or berate yourself for forgetting or finding it difficult. Just start over tomorrow if you forgot to practice today.

Even a two-minute meditation can make a world of difference to your mental well-being.

Remember: Regularity is the key to gaining the full benefit.

THE BENEFITS

There is a great deal of evidence on the benefits of mindfulness meditation based on worldwide psychological and neuroscientific research.

* **It lowers stress**, altering brainwave activity in a positive way;

* **It eases pain** by controlling the volume knob on pain and emotions, benefiting those experiencing chronic pain due to conditions such as arthritis, cancer, and lupus;

* **It calms**, so you are better able to focus, deal with difficulty, and control your reactions to challenging situations;

* **It makes music sound better**, helping you truly enjoy music and sound, enabling you to relax when you hear it;

* **It makes food taste better,** increasing your ability to savour and enjoy food, and as you slow down, you may even naturally consume less;

* **It can help you relate better** to yourself and to others, making you more compassionate;

* **It can help you accept yourself**, making it easier for others to connect with you;

* **It can improve your mental focus**, helping you to study and raising your performance in cognitive and memory tests;

* **It can help improve memory**, acting as a protective force for the brain's neural activities and protecting against memory loss;

* **It can help improve performance** by boosting concentration and confidence;

* **It can help you cope with cancer** by making you calmer and reducing the stress of cancer treatments;

* **It can help with addictive and obsessive thoughts** by short-circuiting repetitive and addictive cycles of obsessional thinking;

* **It can boost your immunity**, increasing your ability to resist colds, flu, and other ailments.

BEING VERSUS DOING

Modern life is all about **DOING**.

"What are you doing today?"

"What are you doing tonight?"

"What are you doing this weekend?"

"What are you doing now?"

We rush to work on trains, on buses, and in cars; and when we are caught in traffic jams or lines, our frustration builds as we cannot get where we are going fast enough.

We save time by eating junk food on the run, at our desks and in cars, even in our homes—there's little or no time to cook or stop to eat with others socially.

We multitask to attack our ever-growing to-do lists, checking our phones as we talk with friends, heads down, eyes glued to the screen, instead of making eye contact or fully engaging with our surroundings and other people.

Mindfulness is about learning to **BE**, not **DO**.

BEING is about:

* walking and looking, hearing—experiencing the air, the light, the view, nature, buildings, people
* sitting quietly
* sitting in the garden and looking at the flowers, the sky, the insects, the clouds, your pets
* watching the river or sea ebb and flow
* lying in bed and taking a few minutes before you rush on with the day
* sitting holding a baby, hugging your child or loved one
* having a pet on your lap, purring warmly
* lying in the sun, eyes closed, breathing, listening to the buzz of a bee

Being is about being, simply, in the moment.

NOW.

LET THIS BOOK BE YOUR GUIDE

This journal will help you practice mindfulness. Whether it is an exercise, a thought-provoking quotation, an illustration, or a lined page for your own notes, the pages of this book offer a small window to help you find daily peace and inner calm. Dip in and out, return to the exercises you like most, and fill the blank pages with your thoughts and doodles.

Take your time. Teaching your mind to calm down takes practice, but you will soon be reaping the benefits. Most importantly: put yourself first. Make time for mindfulness every single day, for the sake of your physical and emotional health. It will improve your relationship with yourself and with those around you.

Enjoy these exercises.

Be mindful.

START THE DAY

A mindful start can help you focus and prepare for the busy day ahead. In the morning, give yourself extra time to get ready.

Under the shower, allow yourself to feel the water on your body. Let the heat awaken your muscles and imagine your cares washed away with the water. Smell your shower gel and let the fragrance invigorate you. Briefly turn the water down to cool to set your skin tingling.

When you finish showering, appreciate the feel of the dry towel against your wet skin. Be aware of how clean and refreshed you feel.

Take the time to eat breakfast slowly, without television or radio or email. Even if it's just fruit or toast, savor at least one part of it. Feel the texture and taste in your mouth.

Check that you have what you need before you leave the house. Try not to rush. Smile to yourself. Step outside and make your way to work, ready to face the day.

"Inner freedom allows us to savor the lucid simplicity of the present moment, free from the past, and emancipated from the future."

Matthieu Ricard,
Happiness: A Guide to Developing Life's Most Important Skill

MINDFUL WALKING

Taking a simple, short walk during the course of your day can help you order your thoughts.

Walk at a comfortable, regular pace. Breathe regularly in time with your walking rhythm. Swing your arms—not too wide, just enough to relax your shoulders and gather a gentle momentum.

Notice your surroundings: the light of the sky, the pattern of clouds, the shapes of the trees and leaves, the colors of doors, cars, and houses. Feel your feet as they tread on the ground, feel the weight of your arms as they swing by your side. Notice the balance in your spine, and lift your head up as you walk.

Keep your attention on what you see, what you smell, what you hear. Be aware of your whole body walking. Stay present.

"I wandered lonely as a cloud
That floats on high o'er vales
   and hills,
When all at once I saw a crowd,
A host, of golden daffodils . . ."

William Wordsworth,
"I Wandered Lonely as a Cloud"

RACING THOUGHTS

Sometimes our minds race with worry and we can't sleep at night. Instead of gnawing away at a problem, step away from it.

Set your timer for 20 minutes. Sit comfortably in a high-backed chair or lie down. Visualize your thoughts jumping around like jumping beans, bouncing balls, or monkeys flying through the trees. Notice the "buzziness" of the thoughts and watch them moving around. Focus on your breathing, thinking "rising" as you breathe in and "falling" as you breathe out.

Go back to your thoughts: notice whether they have retreated a little. If they are still racing, return to your breathing. Continue to breathe, in and out, and occasionally check on your thoughts, noticing them retreat further each time. Notice any discomfort in your body and breathe into it.

When the timer goes off, stay still for a moment and let your awareness come back slowly. Notice where you are and that your back is supported. All is well.

CREATE A CALM SPACE

Homes are busy places, with people always coming and going. Make sure you create a calm place to meditate or simply sit comfortably and be. Make it in your bedroom, a corner of the living room, or even in the bathroom. Gather the following items:

A high-backed chair, large cushion, bed, or yoga mat.

A light blanket.

A timer (optional).

Candles (optional).

A sign for the door saying "Please don't disturb."

"Turn your face to the sun and the shadows fall behind you."

Māori proverb

DEALING WITH DIFFICULT EMOTIONS

(20 to 30 minutes)

Regrets, losses, resentments, anger, disputes. Whatever the cause, it's important to give your feelings space, and yet not be overwhelmed by them.

Set your timer for 20 minutes or half an hour. Sit comfortably on a high-backed chair or lie down.

Close your eyes and focus on your breathing. Notice how your limbs and solar plexus (below your ribs) feel: notice any areas of discomfort and breathe into them. Continue to breathe steadily, and let your mind settle.

Allow a "difficult" thought to arise, such as a resentment or loss. Allow the thought to be for a moment, then let it go by imagining it as a butterfly fluttering away from you. Bring your awareness back to your breathing. Breathe in and out, deeply.

If the difficult thought remains in your mind, return to it and repeat the step of letting it go like a butterfly. Continue until the thought moves freely away.

Bring your attention back to the center of your forehead, and breathe until the timer goes off.

"Helping people better manage their upsetting feelings—anger, anxiety, depression, pessimism, and loneliness—is a form of disease prevention . . . helping people handle them better could potentially have a medical payoff as great as getting heavy smokers to quit."

Daniel Goleman,
Emotional Intelligence

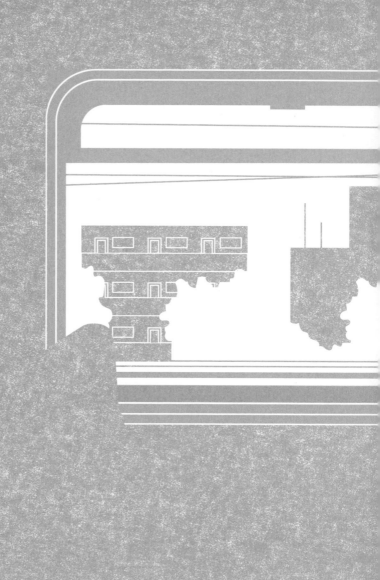

THE COMMUTE

Delays, smells, the crush of fellow passengers, the buzzing of gadgets and music beats: it can all get too much. Look inside yourself for a more soothing experience.

Turn off your gadgets and put away your book. Look around and find a view of scenery passing outside or the flickering lights in the tunnel. Soften your focus. Take a deep breath and exhale.

Close your eyes. Rest your attention on the rhythm of the train and the sounds of doors opening and closing. When people shuffle and move around, let your body flow with the crowd. Make your own inner space behind your eyes and focus on your breathing.

Open your eyes. Return your gaze to the view outside, but don't focus. Be aware of sounds around you and listen out, mindfully, for your stop. When you reach your destination, melt through the crowd and get off.

"In the end, just three things matter: how well we have lived; how well we have loved; how well we have learned to let go."

Jack Kornfield

CALM YOUR NERVES

*Before an interview, an important phone call or presentation,
a little mindfulness can go a long way. I always do this
fifteen-to-twenty-minute meditation before appearing on the
television or radio.*

Find a quiet, private spot where you can be comfortable
for 5 minutes. Sit with your eyes closed. Breathe in and
out, deeply. Notice where the tension is in your body—
butterflies in the stomach, clenched teeth, stiff neck,
wobbly knees, pulsating heart. Breathe deeply, in and out,
five times. Make each breath go deeper than the last.

Squeeze your shoulders up towards your ears, then drop
them. Repeat three times. Breathe. Be aware of your jaw,
your hands, your feet rooted on the ground.

Open your mouth wide, like a cat yawning, then relax it.
Yawn if you can—it's a great tension release. Breathe in,
breathe out. Open your eyes. Smile.

Just before the thing you are dreading, close your eyes and
focus on your breathing. Don't engage in chit-chat with
anyone, or read to "distract" yourself. Smile when you
face your challenge and make eye contact.

ASK FOR WHAT YOU WANT

It can feel very difficult to ask for what you want in any relationship. Perhaps you are afraid of being rejected or judged. Yet it is essential that you feel comfortable about your right to ask.

Stand quietly for a moment and notice what it is you are trying to communicate. Identify your feelings. What sensations do you feel in your body? Tingles? Tensions? Be aware of them.

Clear your mind. Focus on your breath: breathe in and out, deeply. With every out breath, straighten your back and feel taller. With every in breath, feel your chest expand. Feel straighter and more substantial. Feel the solid ground beneath your solid feet.

Now go and ask for what you want.

"To say Hello rightly is to see the other person, to be aware of him as a phenomenon, to happen to him and be ready for him to happen to you."

Eric Berne,
What Do You Say After You Say Hello?

A LONG DAY AT WORK

It's easy to get sucked into the culture of working late at your desk. Regular, mindful breaks can help you de-stress and focus.

Walk mindfully to the restroom or kitchen. Straighten your body, stretch, and notice how you place your feet on the floor one after the other. Notice how your arms swing and how your body feels as you walk.

Back at your desk, take a moment to stretch—feel your arms, legs, fingers, and toes extend fully. Sit back in your chair and roll your head to one side, then the other. Look up to the ceiling and down again. Feel your neck stretching; feel yourself grow taller. Close your eyes and rest them. Exercise your face and mouth by opening your mouth wide, as if you are about to bite an apple or sing. Open your eyes.

Sit up straighter in your chair and feel centered. Go about your work.

COMING HOME

After a full day at work or play, return home and take time to fully "arrive."

Go into your bedroom and close the door. Change out of your clothes into something comfortable, or simply be naked. Lie back spread-eagled on your bed and close your eyes.

Give a big, deep sigh. Notice the places in your body that are aching, tired, hot or cold, sore or rested. Breathe in deeply and feel your lungs fill. Breathe out, blowing the air through your lips. Repeat.

Stretch out further. Reach out your arms and legs, wiggle your fingers and toes. Notice where your mind goes, turning over events from the day, and let the thoughts go like leaves in the wind. Breathe in and out, deeply, exhaling loud and long.

Listen to the sounds of the house and the world outside, and let them go. Breathe in and out, deeply, exhaling loud and long again.

Open your eyes. Notice the light and become aware of your surroundings.

"If you want others to be happy, practice compassion. If you want to be happy, practice compassion."

Dalai Lama

MISUNDERSTANDINGS

Relationships can get fraught when each person assumes the other "should" be able to understand them without explanation. In fact, we have to educate our partners, friends, and family about who we are. Try this exercise before calmly opening a discussion.

Sit somewhere comfortable and breathe in and out.
Put your focus on your breath. Feel your heart and lungs grow with every in breath. Feel warmer and more open as you breathe.

Think compassionately about the other person. Identify two things about them to be thankful for. Notice any negative feelings and let them be, but don't focus on them. Stay here in the moment, with the reasons to be thankful. Accept that their view is different from yours. Respect it.

"A big part of love is forgiveness. In fact, it is impossible for us to love unless we *do* forgive—over and over again."

Louis Proto,
Be Your Own Best Friend: How to Achieve Greater Self-Esteem, Health, and Happiness

WAITING IN LINE

At some point or another, life will lead you to a line and make you wait. Use the time to cultivate mindfulness.

As you stand in line, notice the feelings that are bubbling up—anger, frustration, irritation, boredom. What is going through your mind? What is going on in your body? Do you feel any impulses rising?

Breathe; feel the ground beneath your feet. Breathe again, more deeply; be aware of other people. Try not to absorb their irritability or chat. Notice when you move forward in the line, and loosen your body to relax.

Straighten up and stand taller. Bend your knees slightly to relieve your spine. Allow this moment to be what it is. Keep breathing and noticing your breath. Let time pass and feel your body occupy its space.

"Ask yourself whether you are happy, and you cease to be so."

John Stuart Mill,
Autobiography

A POOR NIGHT'S SLEEP

It's hard to face the day after a bad night. Give yourself time to get your mind and body into the right place.

Don't get up straightaway. Lie in bed for 5 minutes. Stretch out into a starfish shape and wiggle your fingers and toes.

Lying on your back, close your eyes and be aware of how your body feels. Become aware of any places that are aching or uncomfortable. Breathe deeply, in and out, thinking "rising" as you breathe in and "falling" as you breathe out. Repeat.

Open your eyes. Stretch again, then sit upright. Look around. Notice three things in the room that you like: an object, a picture, a burst of color. Let your focus rest on each for a moment.

Get up. Stand with feet hip-width apart and stretch your arms over your head, then lower them and shake out your arms and legs.

Take a deep breath, in and out. You are ready to face the day.

"In today's rush we all think too much, seek too much, want too much and forget about the joy of just Being."

Eckhart Tolle

A MINDFUL SNACK

It's very easy to eat without awareness at work. People bring in cakes and chips, chocolate and sweets, and you might snack all day through boredom or habit. Try this exercise to make yourself more aware of food and more appreciative of your senses.

Find a place to sit with your snack. This could be some raisins, a single square of chocolate, or a strawberry. Look at it, then close your eyes. Focus on your breath and tune out any noise or movement nearby. Breathe in and out. With every out breath, feel more relaxed.

With your eyes still closed, pop your raisins, square of chocolate, or strawberry in your mouth. Let it sit on your tongue. Feel the texture, taste the sweetness, the flavor. Roll it around on your tongue or let it melt. Don't chew. Take time to savor the taste and all the different flavors and textures that are released.

Enjoy every second for as long as you can. Chew and swallow. Open your eyes.

DECISIONS, DECISIONS

Sometimes we simply can't make our minds up. We can procrastinate, toss and turn at night, and discuss at length, but in the end we need to let the decision make itself.

Write down a list of pros and cons about the decision. Put the piece of paper away and sit comfortably in a quiet place. Close your eyes.

Breathe in and out. Deepen your breathing, letting air fill your lungs. Let your mind wander to the issue, but don't fixate on it. Let the matter float past you. Continue to breathe in, then out.

Notice parts of your body that feel tense: your solar plexus (below your ribs)? Your jaw? Your back and shoulders? Visualize breathing into these places and expelling tension with every out breath. Open your eyes and let your thoughts flow again.

Take a new piece of paper and ask yourself: what do I think about the decision? Write down your first thought.

Trust this process. The decision will make itself.

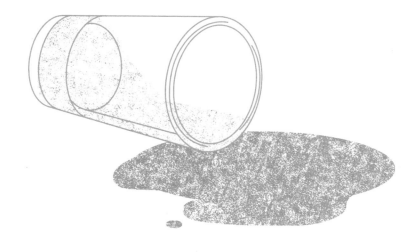

DISAPPOINTMENT

Feelings of disappointment are similar to feelings of loss.
We feel the loss of what could have been, something that was
promised but not delivered. Take your focus away from the
pain by moving it to something benign.

Make yourself comfortable and breathe steadily. Put your
attention behind the midpoint of your forehead.

Bring your mind to the disappointing issue. See it from
a distance and watch your body react to it, but don't be
absorbed in the feelings.

Move away from those feelings and bring your attention
to your left hand. Focus on your thumb. Look at its shape,
the curve of the nail, the creases in the skin. Look at the
space between your thumb and forefinger, and all the
spaces between your fingers. Keep breathing. Stay in this
moment.

"Ah, my Beloved, fill the cup
   that clears
Today of past regrets and
   future fears.
Tomorrow? Why, tomorrow
   I may be
Myself, with Yesterday's Sev'n,
   Thousand Years."

Edward FitzGerald,
The Rubáiyát of Omar Khayyám

DISPEL BLAME

Blaming is powerless behavior, and we all do it. We need to take responsibility for our part in things, realize we are angry, and release the poisonous feeling.

Sit comfortably and breathe in and out, steadily. Focus on your breathing.

Notice the "angry" feelings in your body. Locate them. Are they in your gut? Your lower back? The back of your throat? Identify the color, form, and texture of these feelings. Move towards your anger, but don't embrace it. Be aware of it, its form and location in your body.

Focus on your breathing and deepen it. Let your anger "be." Sit with it.

Blame will not alter these feelings. Let them exist in you and burn down.

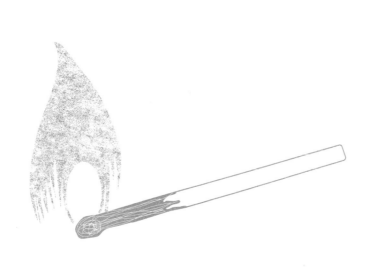

"You don't get to choose how you're going to die. Or when. You can only decide how you're going to live. Now."

Joan Baez,
Daybreak

AT THE BUS STOP

Wind, rain, or sun—the bus will come when it comes. Meanwhile, try this little exercise.

Look around you. Do trees line the road? Are there clouds in the sky? What draws your attention—can you see flowers, shops, office buildings, cars, children? Do people rush or stroll? Or is there nothing to see at all?

Breathe in and breathe out, feeling calmer with every out breath. Stand comfortably, bending your knees slightly. Notice where any tension lies in your body and put your mind to work relaxing each muscle in turn by tensing first, then relaxing.

Know that somewhere a bus is moving towards you. Breathe calmly and watch for your bus.

"I never worry about the future.
It comes soon enough."

Albert Einstein

DECLUTTER

Cabinets, attics, and garages can overflow with possessions and their physical presence can clutter your mental space. Bring order to it all.

Choose one area you want to clear—one cabinet, one corner, one box, one pile. Look at it and take it in. Now imagine that cluttered place clear and clean. See it empty.

Breathe in and out, deeply, three times. Close your eyes. Imagine yourself starting to clear the place, sorting the objects you need from the objects you don't, putting things in bags and bins. Little by little the space will clear. As the objects are removed, feel the space increase in your mind.

Open your eyes. Begin.

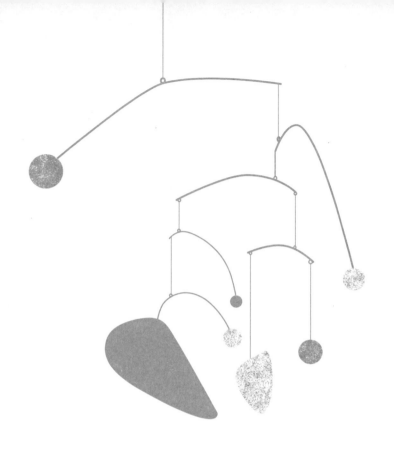

ACCEPTING CHANGE

Change is unsettling. Sometimes it is necessary, but that does not make it welcome. Deal with the difficult feelings by taking your mind to a calm, centered place.

Sit comfortably and breathe in and out, eyes closed.
Be aware of your breath and the position of your body.
Feel the points of pressure on your body: feel your arms by your side or folded in your lap, your feet on the ground.

Visualize the change that has occurred. Imagine the consequences, at work or at home, the objects and people involved. Observe any feelings that rise up.

Return to your breathing. Be aware that you have not changed. Feel the same pressures on your body—the position of your arms, your feet on the ground. Continue to breathe, in and out. Feel relaxed and focused.

Open your eyes.

"Suffering is perfectly natural . . . it is not always the pain *per se* but the way we see it and react to it that determines the degree of suffering we experience. And it is the suffering we experience the most, not the pain."

Jon Kabat-Zinn,
*Full Catastrophe Living: How to Cope with Stress,
Pain and Illness Using Mindfulness Meditation*

SELF-ESTEEM

Self-esteem is an internal judgment of your own worth based on your emotions. Boost your self-esteem and find inner confidence with this simple exercise.

Sit comfortably and close your eyes. Focus on your breath. Breathe in and out, deeply and steadily.

Bring your attention to your torso, your lungs and heart. Imagine yourself opening up. Think to yourself *I am completely good* and *I am completely lovable.* Continue to breathe steadily. Imagine yourself shining with golden light. The more open you feel, the more light you shine.

Prevent any negative thoughts from settling in your mind. Focus on being and accepting yourself.

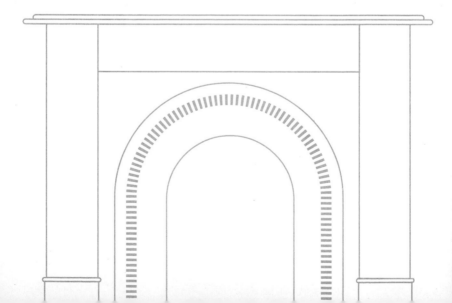

DELAYS

Sometimes we have to wait longer than we expect—delays, broken promises, and time wasted waiting for deliveries can leave us frustrated. Don't let the situation claim your inner calm.

Stand in an A-frame: with your feet apart and your arms by your sides. Breathe in and out, making a hissing noise through your teeth as you push the air out using your solar plexus—the place under your ribs. Repeat, hissing as you exhale.

Raise your arms over your head and stretch upwards. Wiggle your fingers and thumbs, then bring your arms back down to your sides. Breathe in and out, hiss again.

Bring your attention to your surroundings. What looks pleasing today? Notice any colors, plants, pictures, and furniture around you. Breathe.

Become aware of this waiting time as free time, a gift. What can you do right now?

"One night, after a meditation class, I was sitting alone in an empty Tube carriage in London. A man got on, and when the doors closed, he stood in front of me and shouted,

'Give me your money!'

For some reason, I felt calm and relaxed, and I looked up at him, smiled, and said,

'No.'

He looked perplexed and raised his voice:

'Gimme your money!'

I have no idea what possessed me, but I felt invincible and happy that evening, even though I was a woman alone in a train carriage, and we were between stations.

'No,'

I said, and smiled. To my surprise, he
sat down next to me suddenly
and said,

'So you're not giving me your money?'

'Nope,'

I said lightly.

'OK, then,'

he said, and as the train drew into
the station and the doors opened, he
got up and left. I was amazed at my
relaxed fortitude, and surprised that
I'd stood up to him, especially alone,
but I hadn't felt threatened, and I
guess it showed."

Corinne Sweet

A GOOD PLACE

Before you enter a daunting situation—perhaps an annual assessment at work, or meeting your partner's friends for the first time—make sure you are in "a good place," so you can "hear" what is said to you and respond appropriately.

Stand with your body in the shape of an "X": plant your feet firmly on the ground, slightly more than hip-width apart, and hold your arms straight out with palms down. This pose gives you confidence and energy and makes you feel grounded and purposeful.

Lengthen your spine and raise the top of your head, imagining you are being pulled upwards from the crown by a string. Keep your knees slightly bent to relieve your lower back. Tuck your tailbone under.

Breathe in and out, slowly, five times. Feel more grounded with every out breath.

COOKING MINDFULLY

Embrace the sensual nature of preparing food by doing it mindfully.

Gather the ingredients for your meal. Appreciate the different shapes, sizes, and textures: notice the difference between the solid glass bottles and the cooking liquids inside them, and compare these to the colors and organic shapes of fresh vegetables and herbs. Smell the fresh ingredients.

Clear a space and gather your kitchen tools. Take a vegetable and peel it, noticing the color, the feel, and the moisture. Slice and chop it, paying attention to the juices, the sound, the shapes you make. Repeat.

Heat some oil in your pan and add your ingredients. Stir. Watch how the food changes in texture. Look at the colors—a dot of green here, a sliver of orange there. Listen to the sound of moisture being released and the sizzle of heat.

When your meal is ready, stand back and admire your handiwork.

"When you drink, just drink,
When you walk, just walk."

Zen saying

DRIVING WITH CHILDREN

It's a long, hot journey, and the kids are squabbling in the back of the car. Try this exercise when you run out of patience.

Pull into a service station or a parking space. Take a moment to breathe. Breathe deeply, being aware of the air going in and out, for ten breaths. Get out of the car. Get the children out of the car. Imagine all the tension leaving the car with you and dispersing in the air.

Walk to the restroom or to get refreshments. Give the children a break in the fresh air. Breathe, look up at the sky, and encourage the children to burn off their frustration by stretching their legs.

Return to the car, bringing the fresh air and a clear mind back with you. Drive on.

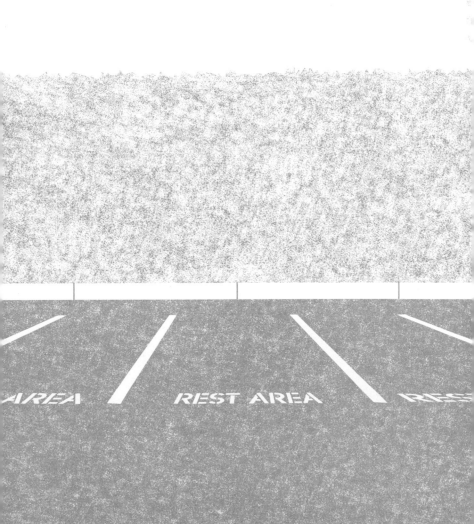

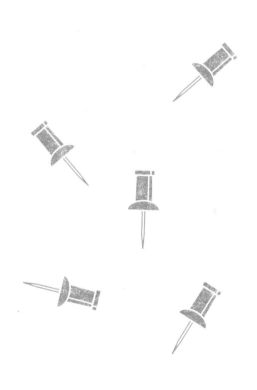

CRITICISM

It is easy to get defensive when criticized and to react or withdraw. Use mindfulness to tame your feelings.

Take a moment to mentally remove yourself from the situation. Breathe. As you breathe in, be aware of the present moment. All is well.

Imagine the opinions of others floating past you, positive and negative. Notice that you are breathing safely and comfortably, that you are not under attack.

Stay in the present moment. Don't think about events that have just passed or what will happen next. An opinion does not condemn you, and you don't have to agree or defend yourself.

Notice your body. Release any tense muscles. Stretch your arms up and shake off any tension. Let the critical words in, hear them, but don't react. Let them go.

Live through this awkward moment and accept that people have different views. If there is something to learn from the criticism, it will emerge. Keep breathing, in and out, until you feel calm.

"Your pain is the breaking of
   the shell that encloses your
      understanding . . .
And you would watch with
   serenity through the winters of
      your grief.
Much of your pain is self-chosen.
It is the bitter potion by which
   the physician within you heals
      your sick self.
Therefore trust the physician,
   and drink his remedy in silence
      and tranquillity."

Kahlil Gibran,
The Prophet

LOOK OUTSIDE

When you find your focus waning, find a window with a view and try this exercise.

Stand or sit comfortably near a window and look outside. Do you see street or sky? Look up and down so you can see both. Identify the fastest-moving object in your vision and the slowest-moving object in your vision. Consider everything moving in your eye line while you are still.

Breathe in and out, and be aware of how you are sitting or standing. If you are standing, bend your knees slightly.

Appreciate this moment.

FLUSTERED

There is always that moment—a slip of the tongue, a
clumsy move—that can expose you to words of ridicule.
Deal with the feelings of embarrassment by breathing through
and over them.

Breathe in and out steadily, experiencing every breath.
Let your feelings roll over you: experience them, but don't
let them flood you.

Close your eyes briefly and imagine being covered by a
psychic shield, like a film draped over you from the head
down. Give it a color, like purple or blue. Visualize it as
a solid, strong reality.

Be aware of your breath coming in and going out. Look
at the source of your feelings. Consider whether someone
is trying to make themself feel better by making you feel
bad. Behind your shield, remove yourself from being a
target.

Continue to breathe in and out. Notice another person or
object in your environment with which you can connect.
Feel the moment and move on to the next one.

"I was always looking outside myself for strength and confidence but it comes from within. It is there all the time."

Anna Freud

A MINDFUL SWIM

Merge aerobic exercise with meditation by learning to swim mindfully.

Carefully lower yourself into the pool and let your body adjust to the temperature. Feel the support and pressure of the water. Take a deep breath and exhale slowly. Start swimming your favorite stroke.

Notice your breathing, thinking "in" as you breathe in and "out" as you breathe out. Feel how your lungs grow and shrink as you move through the water.

Find a comfortable pace. If you are counting lengths, count, but continue to focus on your breathing and keep the pace steady. Feel how easily the water flows over your body. Be aware of your limbs: how they meet gentle resistance with each stroke, and how gracefully your body moves forward.

When you finish, remain in the water, unmoving, eyes closed. Be aware of your body, strong and warm from the exercise, and now soothed by the water as you rest. Notice how you feel as you get out of the water, mindfully.

"I am grateful for what I am and have. My thanksgiving is perpetual. It is surprising how contented one can be with nothing definite—only a sense of existence."

Henry David Thoreau

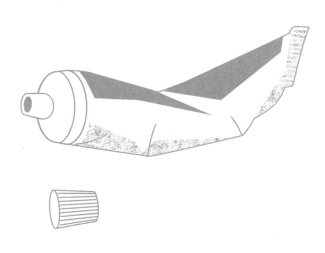

SHARING YOUR SPACE

Living with other people and their habits is often challenging. Quell your irritation with this exercise.

Move away from the source of irritation. Find a quiet place to sit and close your eyes. Focus on your breathing.

Be aware of your body. Feel where you are tense, and focus your breath on these places. Relax as you breathe. Imagine the issue you are irritated by and let it float away from you.

Continue breathing in and out, bringing your attention to the center of your forehead. See your irritation for what it is: a momentary feeling of irritation. Simply let it pass. Open your eyes.

When you can feel the emotion without heat, address the issue with a simple conversation.

THE SAME OLD ARGUMENT

All relationships have tricky areas which you can slip up on again and again. It might be an old disagreement or a sore subject that still needs addressing. Recognize your banana skins and step around them.

When you approach a familiar argument, pause. Notice the well-worn path and the disputes that always lead to discord. Recall the feelings of this place. Do you want to go there again?

Tell yourself to stop. Remove yourself and approach it later from another path. It may take you to a different place.

"All my possessions for a moment of time."

Last words of Elizabeth I

THE NIGHT BEFORE A BUSY DAY

Here are some tips for calming your anxieties mindfully.
Have some pen and paper ready.

Set aside 5 minutes before bed to sit comfortably. Close
your eyes and let yourself relax. Breathe, and watch your
breathing. Notice where the feelings are in your body—
perhaps butterflies in the stomach or mind racing.

Open your eyes and write a list of what you need to do to
prepare for the next day. Write down everything—empty
your brain of all that is filling your mind. Put the list aside
and return to your breathing. When your mind wanders,
bring it back to the center of your forehead.

Open your eyes. Look at your list and calmly do the
things you need to, one at a time.

Feel calm, ready, and prepared for the day to come.

"Remember, when life's path is steep, to keep an even mind."

Horace,
Odes

WASHING UP

Turn a household chore into mindful activity.

Run the water. Add dish soap and observe the bubbles appearing in the running water. Smell the scent; listen to the water gush.

Pick up a dirty plate. Feel the hard dishware in your hands. Take a sponge and wash the plate clean. See the water foam, hear the squeak of sponge against the plate and the sound of cups and plates shifting in the water. Focus on the physical act of making dirty things clean. Rinse. See how the clean dishes shine. Leave it to drain.

Notice that the job does not take long. Admire your handiwork. Feel pleasure at a job well done.

"Mindfulness isn't an uptight I-want-to-shut-everything-out feeling . . . Being mindful is to fully engage with your activity so that it becomes an expression of your true self."

Robert Allen,
365 Pep Talks from Buddha

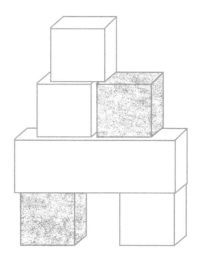

REJECTION

It happens to everyone at some point: you don't get picked for a team; you get left out of a social event; everyone goes out for lunch except you. So how can you handle feeling the odd one out?

Breathe in, breathe out. Know that you are fine as you are, in this moment. Understand that people do and say things for many different reasons, it's not always about you.

Sit with your feelings for a few minutes. Notice what emotions are bubbling under the surface. What do these feelings tell you? Can you locate them in your body?

Breathe slowly. Close your eyes and visualize a place where you feel safe, comfortable, and confident. See yourself there in your mind's eye. Identify any negative thoughts about yourself, but don't let them crowd your mind. Remember three things you like about yourself. Make ample space for them. Hold on to this space and open your eyes.

Remember that life is long. There will always be another opportunity, another event. You could organize the next one.

"I have come from having suicidal thoughts in the depths of my despair, to arriving at a point in my life where I have never been stronger, and I look forward to the future, and whatever it has in store for me. You can, too, whatever your circumstances."

Angie Buxton-King,
The NHS Healer: How My Son's Life Inspired a Healing Journey

BREAKING POINT

The home can be a refuge, but it is also the busy center of family life. If you feel overwhelmed by the constant demands of parenting, caring, or household chores, it is essential to give yourself a break.

Find somewhere to go and be alone, and close the door if possible. Sit or lie down comfortably and breathe deeply, in and out, five times. Whenever you breathe out, blow out your breath through pursed lips.

Allow yourself to feel anger or frustration. Notice where it exists in your body—in your clenched jaw, your hunched shoulders, or the pit of your stomach. Let your emotions rise, and watch them peak. Imagine riding your emotion like an ocean wave. Watch yourself from the outside. Let the emotion carry you, let it rise. Now let it fall.

Breathe in to the emotion, unclench your jaw, straighten your shoulders, and release your stomach muscles. Feel more centered with every breath.

Let yourself be with the difficult emotion, without judgment. Know the feeling will pass.

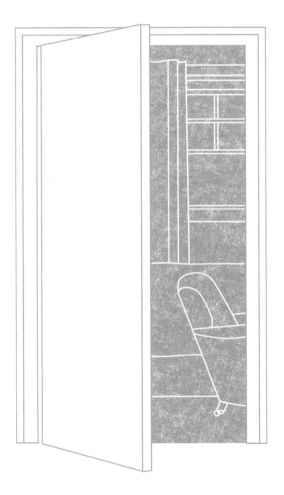

"The presence of thoughts is more important than our subjective judgment of them. But neither must these judgments be suppressed, for they are also existent thoughts which are part of our wholeness."

Carl G. Jung,
Memories, Dreams, Reflections

EAT OUTSIDE

Try to get away from your desk and take your lunch outside. Even five minutes in the fresh air will make all the difference to the day.

Find a good spot to sit—a park bench, a low wall, a table outside a café. Unwrap your lunch and look at it. Consider the color, shape, and texture of your food. Consider the care taken in its preparation.

Take a bite; feel and taste every mouthful. As you eat, be aware of the fresh air on your skin and in your lungs.

After you've eaten, spend a few minutes watching people go by. Resist the temptation to check your phone or hurry back.

Just be.

A CHILD'S BEDTIME

Try this exercise when your exhausted child simply won't go to sleep.

Get your child into bed. Dim the lighting and turn off gadgets and music. Sit next to the bed and tell them you're going to play a sleeping game. Ask them to close their eyes and breathe steadily. Count with them each breath in and out.

Tell them to imagine sinking safely and comfortably into the bed, pretending it is a giant marshmallow. Talk them through each part of their body sinking deeper and deeper into their comfy marshmallow, starting at the toes and working up the body through the legs, knees, thighs, tummy, fingers, arms, chest, and neck, finishing at the top of the head.

They may fall asleep before you get to the end.

SITTING IN TRAFFIC

Whether you're the driver or the passenger, take a moment to relax.

Turn off the radio. If you are driving, notice how you are holding the steering wheel—loosen the grasp of one hand and flex your fingers. Return your hand to the wheel and loosen and flex the other hand. Breathe in and breathe out, exhaling noisily.

Check your shoulders, back, neck, and face for tension. Roll your head from side to side, up and down. Shrug your shoulders up to your ears and release. Repeat.

Notice how far forward or back you are in your seat—are you hunched over? Relax a little. Notice your feet and legs—if stationary, put the hand brake on and let your feet rest on the floor. Breathe. Check the mirror and be aware of the other cars and the people in them. Be poised to move physically and mentally. Tell yourself: "I have all the time in the world."

Keep breathing. Consciously unclench your hands and hold the steering wheel lightly. Stay aware, but relaxed, as you move forward slowly. You will get there in the end.

"If you're walking down the right path and you're willing to keep walking, eventually you'll make progress."

Barack Obama

THE MINDFUL GARDENER

Gardening literally puts us in touch with nature and is wonderfully soothing for overheated minds, bodies, and souls. It's easy to be mindful when your hands are in the dirt.

Choose a simple task that you enjoy, like sowing seeds, thinning out seedlings, weeding, or cutting the grass. Wear gloves if you like—though it's better if you don't.

Notice the texture of the soil, the smells, and the colors. If there are flowers, notice the stage of their flowering. Have the buds fully opened? Focus on physical sensations: what you see, feel, and hear. Be present.

Be aware of your body: where you are bending and which muscles are doing the work. When your body tells you to stop, take a break.

Notice the green shoots coming out of the earth, the freshly unfurling leaves, and the rich soil on your hands. Stay in the present, and enjoy your partnership with nature.

"Some of nature's most exquisite handiwork is on a miniature scale, as anyone knows who has applied a magnifying glass to a snowflake."

Rachel Carson,
The Sense of Wonder

MONEY

Money can bring up strong feelings. Making it, keeping it, and having enough can preoccupy our thoughts. Take a mindful attitude to monetary wealth.

Consider how money comes into your life. Now consider what money brings you. How much do you need it all?

Meditate on the things you appreciate in life. Notice what is reliant on money, and what is not.

Breathe deeply, in and out. Focus on your breathing for five breaths. Consider the air in your body and the money in your wallet. Consider what you want more of and what you need more of.

Be grateful for all that you have.

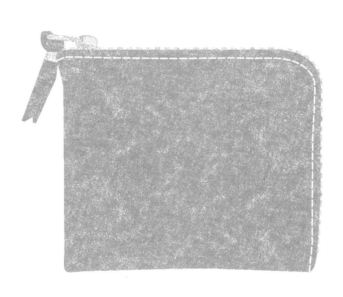

LIFE'S LITTLE IRRITATIONS

Litter-dropping, line-jumping, automated phone systems, and bad drivers—little things can drive us, literally, to distraction. Instead of upping the ante, try this meditation.

Stand on an escalator, on the correct side, and be aware of people passing.

Pick up a piece of litter someone drops and put it in the trash can with your negative thoughts.

If you hear someone shout in a moment of road rage, let it flow over you.

If you need a seat on a bus or a train, ask someone politely if they'd be so kind as to let you sit down.

Walk through a door and hold it open for someone behind you.

Ask for what you need or want—a glass of water, a window to be opened.

Forgive lateness or delay by using the time to appreciate your surroundings.

Let these little, unimportant things happen around you, and just be.

"The generations of living things pass in a short time, and like runners, hand on the torch of life."

Lucretius,
De Rerum Natura

COPING WITH GRIEF AND LOSS

Loss is painful. Whether it's the death of a loved one or the loss of opportunities, objects, or dreams, the challenge is to accept that grief is part of life, and to live every moment well.

Remember good and happy times. Remind yourself of the things you loved about or wanted from what you have lost. Admit your grief. Feel it.

Enjoy every second of life while it is still with you. Hold hands, kiss, touch, look at a flower, pat the dog, make memories, enjoy the light.

Be thankful for what you had while you had it.

"Watching a peaceful death of a human being reminds us of a fallen star; one of a million lights in a vast sky that flares up for a brief moment only to disappear into the endless night forever."

Elisabeth Kübler-Ross,
On Death and Dying

REVIVE

A basic tenet of looking after yourself is to rest when you are weary, sleep if you are tired. Even a five- or ten-minute nap can make all the difference. At home or at work, you might find an empty office; in the warm months, find a park where you can lie down.

Find a space to lie down comfortably, alone if possible. Rest your head on a folded-up sweater for insulation and comfort. Set a timer for 5 or 10 minutes.

Close your eyes and let your body sink into the ground. Stretch your arms out to the side, widen your legs slightly, and stretch your fingers and toes. If you have back problems, bend your knees and put your feet flat on the ground, hip-width apart, pressing your lower back gently to the floor. Breathe in and out, deeply and steadily.

Place your hands lightly under your ribs and feel the air going in and out. Keep your attention focused in the middle of your forehead, but notice sounds around you, smells, movements.

When your timer goes off, stretch your hands above your head. Lie still for a moment before getting up.

"Life is not complex. We are complex. Life is simple, and the simple thing is the right thing."

Oscar Wilde

ENDINGS

All good things come to an end. Whether you're experiencing the end of a job, a relationship, or a friendship, let this exercise comfort and energize you.

Lie down in a quiet place, with your back straight and arms lying slightly away from your body. Support your lower back with a small cushion or rolled-up towel if necessary. Breathe in and out.

Bring your knees up to your chest and put your arms around your shins. Keeping your spine in contact with the floor, roll your knees over to the right and then to the left, and then move your knees around in a gentle circular movement. Be aware of your breathing throughout. Don't struggle. If holding your shins feels too hard on your back, hold on to your thighs instead.

Relax your body into the floor as you rock and roll. Be aware of yourself alone, in this moment. Stay aware of your breathing.

Release your legs and gently lower one and then the other to the ground. Rest.

BE LOVED

Loving someone is all about acceptance, acknowledging their differences, and appreciating them. To love someone well, you have to love yourself well, too.

Notice three things you like about yourself. Write them down. Meditate on them.

Appreciate everything that you are, now, in the present.

TOO MUCH TO DO

Your to-do list is enormous and growing every minute. Where do you start?

Write a new list of the top ten things you need to do— list more than ten things if they are pressing. Fold the piece of paper and put it away for the moment. Set your timer for 5 or 10 minutes.

Close your eyes and breathe in and out, focusing on the breath. Imagine a clean desk with everything in neat piles, each pile representing a task. Breathe in, hold for three counts; breathe out, hold for three counts. Notice any places of tension in your body and let them go, one by one.

Allow thoughts of your list to float into your mind. Watch them go past—don't hold on to them. Notice your breathing again, and gently pull your attention back to behind your forehead when your mind wanders.

Envision your desk again with neat, orderly piles, all sorted. Continue to breathe in and out.

Open your eyes and come to, mindfully, and let the first thought pop into your head. Trust that this is the place to start on your list.

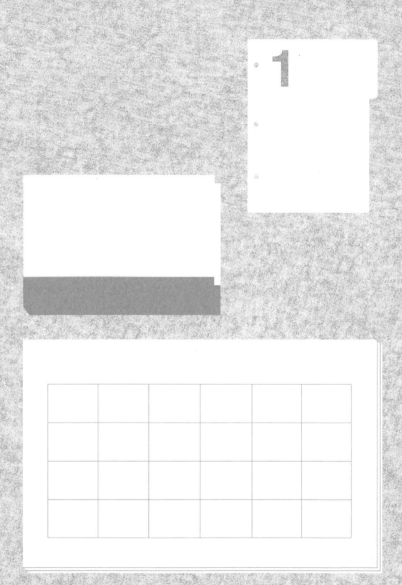

"Practice not-doing, and everything will fall into place."

Lao Tzu,
Tao Te Ching

BAD NEWS

We look for the good things in life but inevitably encounter the bad things, too. Bad news can shock the system, make us numb and silent or loud and angry. Use this exercise to process your emotions.

Lie down comfortably or sit in a high-backed, supportive chair. Cover yourself with a light blanket. Breathe in and out, deeply. Notice your breath coming in through your nose and out through your mouth.

Feel the way your body sits or lies, notice where your body is in contact with the bed, floor, or chair. Know that you are safe and warm. In this moment, nothing can harm you. Continue to take deep, steady breaths.

Let your attention go to the news. Imagine being held and supported as you take in the information, gently. Absorb it and sit with it. It exists and so do you.

Say to yourself "All is well." Repeat this in your mind as you breathe. Stay with your sense of taking in the news, repeating "All is well" if you feel overwhelmed.

Open your eyes and allow yourself to rest for a few minutes.

"Nothing happens to any man that he is not formed by nature to bear."

Marcus Aurelius,
Meditations

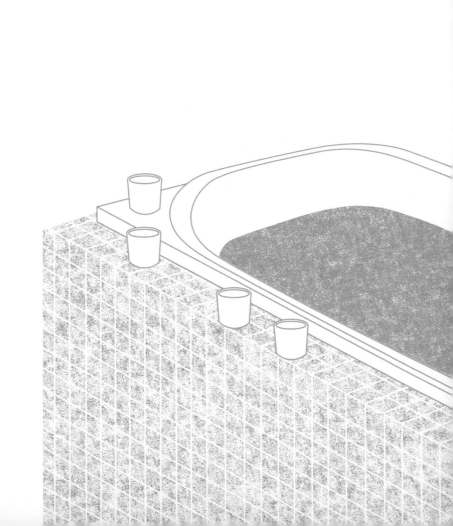

A MINDFUL BATH

Run a bath and add your favorite bath oil. Light some candles if you wish. Adjust the temperature of the water and step in.

Lie back in the bath and feel the water envelop your body. Give yourself over to sensation. Notice the temperature of the water and the smooth surface of the bath. Lift out an arm and watch the water run off it. Breathe deeply into your stomach. Stay in the moment.

Stay in the bath, just feeling the heat and watching the steam rise. Add more hot water when you need to and feel the heat flood in and around you.

Empty your mind of thoughts and tasks and stay focused on sensation. Revel in the experience.

SENSORY OVERLOAD

*Open-plan offices, ringing phones, tapping keyboards, the
smell of food and drink . . . If the atmosphere of your
workplace is getting to you, try this exercise.*

Scan your office for something to look at that is
calming—this could be a plant in a pot, a picture on the
wall, a paperweight, or another benign object on your
desk. Take a moment to look at the object, really look at
it. Take in its beauty, color, rhythm. Visually trace its lines,
sense the weight of it and the space it claims in the room.

Turn your attention back to yourself. Notice the space
you claim in the room. Sit up straight and take a deep
breath. Exhale. Return to your work with more focus.

When you next feel your senses assailed, turn your
attention to the same object and breathe through it.

"Only when you drink from the river of silence shall you indeed sing."

Kahlil Gibran,
The Prophet

FIND YOURSELF

*Families are cauldrons of need and demand. Whether you're
a parent or a caretaker for older relatives, sometimes you
can feel at the beck and call of everyone else. Make time for
yourself.*

Find a quiet corner in your home where you can be
undisturbed for 10 minutes. Sit comfortably or lie down.
Close your eyes. Focus on the sound and rhythm of your
own breathing.

Listen to the sounds of the household and let them wash
over you like a wave. Hear the voices and noises, but don't
let your focus drift to them. Keep your focus on yourself.
Accept the sounds of the household and acknowledge
the people connected to them. Be aware that you are an
important part of the household, too.

Breathe deeply. Become aware of yourself, and the space
you occupy now. Think to yourself *All is well* and *I can
cope with anything.*

Continue to breathe, deeply, for a few minutes. Return to
the fray.

CONFRONTATION

No matter what side you are on, the hostility of conflict will unsettle your emotions. Take time to recover.

Remove yourself from the scene and find a quiet place— an empty room, a stairwell, a bathroom. Take time to tune in to yourself. Feel your feelings. Breathe deeply.

If you feel angry, outraged, or guilty, let the feelings ripple through you. Breathe into them. Notice how you are standing. Are your shoulders slouched? Open them out, stand taller. If your mind is racing, calm it by focusing on something positive about yourself—your hair, your height, your voice.

Observe your breathing. Is it shallow or fast? Take a deep breath and exhale. Repeat until your breathing is steady.

Notice if your feelings have eased. Continue to stand tall and breathe deeply until you can feel your irritated feelings without being overpowered by them.

"I believe that we should confront death as we confront other fears. We should contemplate our ultimate end, familiarize ourselves with it . . . Staring into the face of death, with guidance, not only quells terror but renders life more poignant, more precious, more vital."

Irvin D. Yalom,
Staring at the Sun: Overcoming the Dread of Death

ON THE BUS

Even a short hop is an opportunity for meditation.

Turn your attention to a door or window. Look up and out. Watch the world outside moving past—sky, trees, shops, houses, street lights, people. Breathe.

Consider the space your body inhabits. Be aware of the firm floor beneath your feet and the air above your head. Consider the space the bus inhabits as it travels towards your destination. Accept that the journey will take the time it takes. Close your eyes and breathe in and out. Repeat. Let the chatter or proximity of people wash over you.

Open your eyes and focus on the scenery outside. Relax and listen for your stop.

PATIENCE

People, circumstances, and your own teenage children can test your fortitude. Shore up your patience with this standing meditation.

Take up the Mountain pose from Yoga: stand with legs hip-width apart and arms down by your sides. Keep your head up with neck straight, but not strained. Be comfortable. Breathe in and out, steadily.

Keep breathing. Notice your feet rooted on the ground. Imagine a string pulling your head up gently from the crown, and let your back straighten. Keep your knees slightly bent.

Keep breathing and notice your breath. Feel the air going into your lungs and down into your belly, grounding you further. Continue to take deep breaths in this position until you feel relaxed and stable.

Be aware that you are strong, capable, and grounded. You can deal with anything.

"When I was run over by a ten-ton truck at seventeen and rushed to the hospital, I was put in traction after an emergency operation to save my life. For the next two weeks I experienced extreme agony 24/7 from multiple fractures, spinal damage, puncture wounds . . . I had morphine, but the injections would wear off increasingly quickly. In desperation I began to bite the sheets to control the pain. Then I happened upon something: if I focused on the pain, it disappeared. I began to focus my mind on the pain as a means of controlling it. Instead of trying to blank the pain, I would go into it, flying my mind like a bee into a beehive, and thereby I began to use my conscious mind to help myself survive the agony. Much later, I found out that this is one of the tenets of mindfulness: to focus on the pain, rather than avoid it, to manage it, to ride it, powerfully."

Corinne Sweet

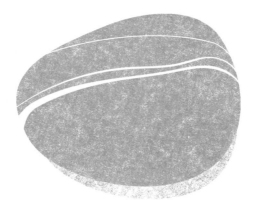

GREEN-EYED MONSTER

Don't let jealous, envious, or competitive feelings eat you up.
Let it go.

Sit in a quiet place and breathe calmly, watching your
breath. Close your eyes, or fix your gaze on the wall.
Imagine your envy as a large pebble. Give it shape and
form. Give it weight and texture. It is heavy, but can be
held in one hand.

Imagine carrying the pebble to a seashore. The tide is
high, the water is by your feet. Raise your arm and throw
the pebble into the sea. Watch it arc into the distance,
then disappear with a SPLASH.

Breathe deeply. Let it go.

UNPACK YOUR SUITCASE

Complete your homecoming from a trip away by meditating as you unpack.

Take a moment to arrive. Don't unpack immediately. Rest in a quiet spot and relax. Spend a few minutes to simply be, back in your home. Notice any irritable thoughts that come to the surface. Let them exist, but don't focus on them.

Take your suitcase to your room and open it. Slowly unpack your belongings, sorting them into piles. Appreciate the colors and textures. Imagine them embodying happy moments and memories from your time away. Savor them.

Put your belongings away until nothing remains. Look at your empty suitcase. Close it. Put the suitcase away, but hold on to the good memories.

Stand up and stretch, then re-engage with the household.

"To become somebody starts with being aware. Being aware starts with standing, or the urge to stand. Standing starts with finding one's ground, which shapes our bodies. This occurs by the development of attitudes which help us to organize our living."

Stanley Keleman,
Your Body Speaks Its Mind

GO TO SLEEP

This guided meditation is a good way to get to sleep, even in the middle of a restless night.

Lying in bed, put your hands on your abdomen, palms down. Close your eyes and breathe in and out. Focus on your breath. Let the bed take your weight. Sink into it.

Flatten your lower back into the bed. Let your jaw loosen and open your mouth wide as if you are about to yawn. If this brings on a real yawn, let it surface.

Bring your attention to your toes, one by one, then the soles of your feet, your ankles, and up to your calves. Move your attention up your body: your knees, thighs, hands. Feel them all heavy on the bed.

Continue upwards, bringing your attention to your solar plexus, under your diaphragm. Let your breath in here several times. Move your attention up your body to the chest area, and think of it widening and opening as air comes in. Move on to your arms: feel that they are heavy and relaxed.

Finally, bring your attention to your neck, face, and head. Allow your mouth to slacken. Feel your head as a heavy weight on the pillow, and your shoulders sinking into the bed.

Drift off to sleep.

THE MINDFUL BODY

Truly appreciate physical sensation by becoming more aware of your own body, its needs and rhythms, its senses and contours.

Lie down comfortably on your back. Breathe in and out, slowly. Feel any tensions in your body and breathe into them. Relax.

Place your hands on your breastbone, palms down, and feel your breath come and go. Notice how your chest rises and falls. Notice how your hands rise and fall with your chest.

Move your hands to your abdomen. Continue to breathe. Notice the heat of your abdomen beneath your hands. Feel the curve of your belly. Stretch one leg and then the other. Feel the surface beneath your limbs. Repeat with your arms.

Become aware of the component parts of your body functioning as a whole in this moment. Appreciate your senses: they enable you to experience the world.

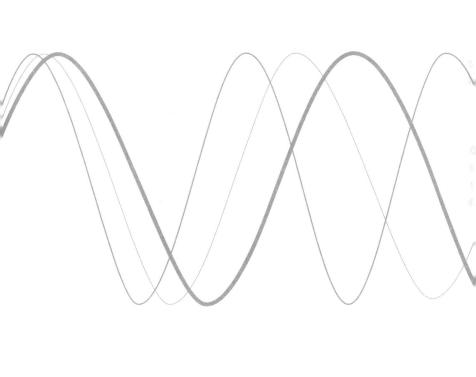

HOLD ON TO A GOOD DAY

Some days at work are great. You achieved what you set out to do, you ticked things off, and you feel good about yourself. Retain this feeling on the journey home.

Be aware of your posture. Whether you are sitting on a train or walking down the street, hold your head up and keep your shoulders relaxed. Be aware of your body.

Look around you. Notice the light, the texture of a person's coat, the trees and sky if you can see them. Find and observe attractive things in your environment. Stay with yourself as you travel, aware of the journey, the changing landscape.

Hold on to your good feelings. Feel them gather in the relaxed parts of your body and travel with you. Say to yourself "I am good" or "All is well" and mean it.

"Life is not the way it's supposed to be. It's the way it is. The way you cope with it is what makes the difference."

Virginia Satir

REGRET

Don't let regret for the past ruin your present.

Make a list of what is good about your life, in the now.
Meditate, thinking about these aspects.

Breathe. Focus on the present, the moment, appreciating
you are alive. Let your mind settle on one of the
regretful thoughts. Imagine regret being like a sandcastle
crumbling into sand, getting blown away by the wind and
washed out to sea.

Let it go.

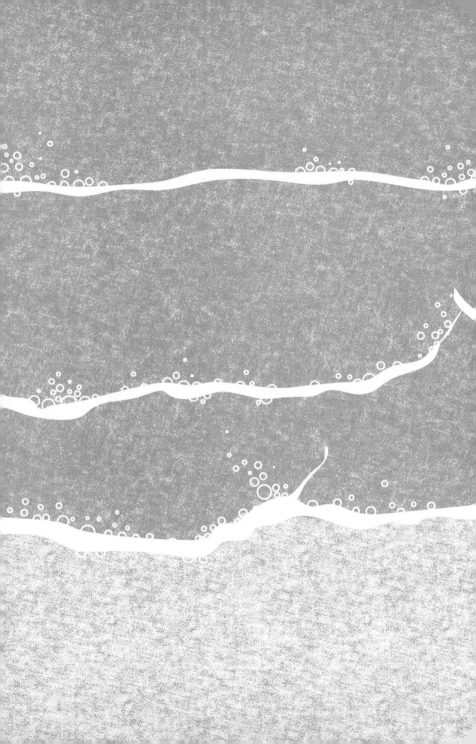

"What's gone and what's past help
Should be past grief."

William Shakespeare,
The Winter's Tale

A FULL LIFE

Mindfulness is about appreciating the small moments as well as the big ones. Try to do two things on this list every day.

Remember three things you love about yourself.

Look for one small thing to appreciate wherever you are—a simple meal, the branch of a tree, the smile on a stranger's face, or the hearty rumble of a passing train.

Focus on breathing out negativity and breathing in positivity.

Be honest with yourself, if no one else.

Make friends with your feelings; don't run away from them.

Live life one day at a time.

"We all age, it is inevitable, and we will all die. Until that moment, every second we are alive, aging is also about living. We should value every day as a gift, always look for the positive and take every opportunity to move, eat, drink, feel, see, and hear. Treasure and value yourself as a unique human being."

Corinne Sweet

NOTES

NOTES

NOTES

REFERENCES FOR QUOTATIONS

Page 25: Matthieu Ricard, *Happiness: A Guide to Developing Life's Most Important Skill* (Atlantic, 2007)

Page 29: William Wordsworth, "I Wandered Lonely as a Cloud"

Page 39: Daniel Goleman, *Emotional Intelligence* (Bloomsbury, 1996)

Page 49: Eric Berne, *What Do You Say After You Say Hello?* (Corgi, 1975)

Page 59: Louis Proto, *Be Your Own Best Friend: How to Achieve Greater Self-esteem, Health and Happiness* (Piatkus, 2002)

Page 63: John Stuart Mill, *Autobiography* (Penguin, 1989)

Page 75: Edward Fitzgerald, *The Rubáiyát of Omar Khayyám* (OUP, 2010)

Page 79: Joan Baez, *Daybreak* (Dial Press, 1968)

Page 83: Albert Einstein, *The Expanded Quotable Einstein* (Princeton University Press, 2000)

Page 89: Jon Kabat-Zinn, *Full Catastrophe Living: How to Cope with Stress, Pain and Illness Using Mindfulness Meditation* (Piatkus, 2013)

Page 107: Kahlil Gibran, *The Prophet* (Pan, 1991)

Page 117: Henry David Thoreau, *Letters to Various Persons* (1865)

Page 127: Horace, *Odes*

Page 131: Robert Allen, 365 *Pep Talks from Buddha* (MQ Publications, 2003)

Page 135: Angie Buxton-King, *The NHS Healer: How My Son's Life Inspired a Healing Journey* (Virgin Books, 2010)

Page 139: Carl G. Jung, *Memories, Dreams, Reflections* (Random House, 1989)

Page 151: Rachel Carson, *The Sense of Wonder* (HarperCollins, 1998)

Page 157: Lucretius, *De Rerum Natura*

Page 161: Elisabeth Kübler-Ross, *On Death and Dying* (Routledge, 2008)

Page 165: Oscar Wilde, Letter to Robert Ross

Page 173: Lao-Tzu, *Tao Te Ching*

Page 177: Marcus Aurelius, *Meditations*

Page 183: Kahlil Gibran, *The Prophet* (Pan, 1991)

Page 189: Irvin D. Yalom, *Staring at the Sun: Overcoming the Dread of Death* (Piatkus, 2011)

Page 201: Stanley Keleman, *Your Body Speaks Its Mind* (Center Press, 1989)

Page 213: William Shakespeare, *The Winter's Tale*

ACKNOWLEDGMENTS

Heartfelt thanks go to Jane Graham Maw of Graham Maw Christie, my literary agent, for keeping me in mindfulness; and to Cindy Chan of Pan Macmillan for excellent editing/ guidance. Also, thanks to therapist colleagues Vicky Abram, ever encouraging, challenging and wonderful; to Debbie Isaacs for your enthusiasm and support; to Alan Pleydell and Lucy West for your personal experience and input; and to Alegra Druce, Dominic Goldberg, Silvia Lautier, Val Lementayer, Ally Burcher, Bob Lentell, Polly Farquharson, Gill Doust, Paul Allsop, Terry Cooper, Oriel Methuen, and all at Spectrum Therapy for wonderful support. Warmest thanks, too, to Sue Pratt and Josine Meijer; and heartfelt thanks also, as ever, to my long-suffering family, Rufus Potter and Clara Potter-Sweet, for your daily love, support, and tolerance. Finally, thanks to Corinne Haynes for your constant encouragement, despite everything.